THE WORD WORKS!

Shirley Greenslade

THE WORD WORKS

AGAPÉ WORD & WORSHIP CENTER
P.O. Box 39172
Solon, Ohio 44139
(216) 248-7667

Printed in the United States

Valley Printing & Graphics, Inc.
Dover, Ohio

9th Printing 2001

Contents and cover may not be reproduced for resale purposes without the express written consent of Agapé Word & Worship Center.

©Copyright 1995
Agapé Word & Worship Center
P.O. Box 39172
Solon, Ohio 44139

All Rights Reserved

TABLE OF CONTENTS

The Word Works	1
Forgiveness	2
Prayer of Forgiveness	2
Putting on the Armor	3
Speaking Words of Faith	4, 5, 6
Grace — Favor	6, 7
Peace	8
Sleep	9
Freedom	9
Obedience	9
Joy	10
Strength	11, 12
Knowledge	12
Spiritual Wisdom and Understanding	13
Spiritual Maturity	14
Spiritual Maturity for Others	15
Life	16
Eternal Life/Salvation	16, 17
Trusting God	18
Hope	19
Righteousness	20
Power	21
Health and Healing	22, 23, 24
Bones	25
Skin	25
Hair	25
Feet	25

Blood 26
Eyes and Ears 26
Teeth 26
Health and Healing Prayer 27
Hurt, Harm and Attack of Enemy 27, 28, 29, 30
Drugs, Alcohol, Nicotine, Addictions 31, 32
Weight Loss — Dieting 32
Fear 33
Staying Out of Strife 34
Love 35, 36
For a Mate 36, 37
Marriage 38
Barrenness and Miscarriage 39
Pregnancy 39, 40, 41
Children 41, 42, 43, 44
Words of Faith for Children 44, 45, 46
Abundance 46
Prosperity 47, 48, 49
Employment 49, 50
Business, etc. 51, 52
For Pastors 53
Praise 53, 54
Victory 54, 55
Protection 56, 57
Using the Blood of Jesus 56, 57
Total Divine Protection
    Psalm 91 .... 57, 58

THE WORD WORKS

This book is the combined effort of several people who have used God's Word and seen It work. It is not a replacement for the Bible, but a topical Scripture reference to help in your immediate situation.

God says in Isaiah 55:10, 11 that as the rain and snow come down from heaven, and do not return, but water the earth and make it bring forth and bud, that it may give seed to the sower and bread to the eater: so shall His Word be that is spoken out of His mouth: It shall not return unto Him void, but It shall accomplish that which He pleases, and It shall prosper in the thing where It is sent.

God loves you and cares about all that concerns you, but in order to help you, He needs you to speak His Word. The Word never fails and as you speak It in faith, the power of the Holy Spirit will be there to bring It to pass.

As we speak, the Word changes things, situations and circumstances in our lives, so they line up with what God's Word says. By speaking only God's Word, we do not give the devil any place to operate in our lives. When we speak our own words, we are snared and overtaken by the enemy. As believers, satan has no place in our lives except when he is given one by the words of our mouths.

Begin Speaking God's Word over every area of your life. Remember, the choice of victory or defeat is yours! Life and death are in the power of your tongue! (Proverbs 18:21)

Start speaking God's Word today and be prepared for victory!

FORGIVENESS

Forgiveness is an important part of our walk with the Lord; it is not an option; it is a command. In His Word, God tells us repeatedly that if we do not forgive others, we will not be forgiven by our Father.

Unforgiveness will stop our prayers from being answered. If we do not forgive others, unforgiveness in our spirits grows into resentment, bitterness and hatred, eventually consuming us. In Matthew 18:21,22 and Luke 17:4, Peter asks Jesus how often we must forgive. Jesus replies 70 X 7 times which is 490 times in a day; allowing 8 hours for sleeping that amounts to forgiving every two minutes. The Lord is showing us that we should be in a constant state of forgiveness.

Colossians 3:13 ... forgive one another; if any man has a quarrel or complaint against you, as Christ forgave you, so you do the same.

Matthew 6:14,15 says if you forgive men their trespasses, your heavenly Father will also forgive you, but if you don't forgive others of the wrong things they do, then neither will your Father in heaven forgive you.

Matthew 18:35 tells us that forgiveness must be from the heart.

PRAYER OF FORGIVENESS

Father, Your Word says unforgiveness will stop my prayers from being answered and give the enemy a place in my life. Your Word also says that if I do not forgive others, neither will You forgive me for the wrong things I have said and done. Right now, in the name of Jesus, I forgive all those who have hurt me, cursed me, used me, condemned me or come against me in any way. I forgive them and set my will to forget those things. I ask that You, in Your mercy and compassion, forgive them as well.

I ask You, Father, to forgive me for the wrong things I have said and done. Forgive me for judging, criticizing or condemning anyone and for anything I have spoken which was contrary to Your Word. By faith, I receive Your forgiveness. I set a watch over my mouth that I may speak only what Your Word says in every situation and circumstance. I set my will to be pleasing to You in everything I do and say. I thank You, Father, for Your forgiveness and Your mercy, and I praise Your glorious Name.

PUTTING ON THE ARMOR

Father, Your Word says in Ephesians 6:12, that we do not wrestle with flesh and blood (people) but against principalities, powers, rulers of darkness and spiritual wickedness in high places. We put on our spiritual armor so we are able to withstand the evil of each day.

We stand having our loins girded with Truth — the truth of Your Word, which is forever settled in heaven. It is the same yesterday, today and forever. We have on our breastplate of righteousness, which is right standing with You. Righteousness gives us the ability to come boldly to Your throne of grace to obtain mercy and find grace to help in our time of need. (Hebrews 4:16)

Our feet are shod with the preparation of the Gospel of Peace; we walk in the power and authority of the mighty name of Jesus at Whose name every knee shall bow in heaven and earth and under the earth. (Philippians 2:9-11)

Above all, we take the shield of faith which quenches all the fiery darts of the wicked. These fiery darts cause us to speak negatively and give satan a place in the situations which we have believed for You to change. As we have our shield up defensively, we ask the Holy Spirit to put a watch over our mouths and help us keep our tongues from evil. (Psalm 34:13) We are determined to speak only what Your Word says.

We take the helmet of salvation through which our every need is met. Salvation gives us the right to receive divine protection according to Psalm 91. Lastly, we take up the sword of the Spirit, which is Your mighty Word, quick, powerful and sharper than any two edged sword. Your Word says the weapons of our warfare are not carnal but mighty through You to the pulling down of the strongholds in our lives. (II Corinthians 10:4)

Now that we are fully "dressed" in Your protection, we stand complete in You expecting victory over every attack of the devil.

As we put Your Word before You with prayer and thanksgiving, Your Words have opportunity to work and perform as You promised!

SPEAKING WORDS OF FAITH

All things are mine, things of men, of the world, of life and death; things present and things to come, all are mine because I am Christ's and He is God's. (I Corinthians 3:21-23)

My mouth speaks God's Word which is in my heart in abundance. (Matthew 12:34)

I let no corrupt communication (anything contrary to God's Word) come out of my mouth. (Ephesians 4:29)

I fix my mind on and speak only those things that are true, honest, just, pure, lovely, praise worthy and of a good report. (Philippians 4:8)

Everything I say and do, I do in the name of Jesus. (Colossians 3:17)

I hold fast to my confession of faith by saying only what the Word says. I do not waver for He that promised is faithful. (Hebrews 4:14; 10:23)

I continually confess God's Word; It does not return to Him void but It accomplishes and prospers as He pleases. (Isaiah 55:11)

I refuse to receive anything contrary to the Word of God. I refuse to speak words contrary to His Word because I am submitted to God. I resist you satan and you must flee from me. (James 4:7)

Because I seek the Lord, I do not want for any good thing. (Psalm 34:10)

I cry, the Lord hears and delivers me out of all my troubles. (Psalm 34:17)

The Word of the Lord stands; what He has spoken He brings to pass; what he has purposed, He does; this gives Him pleasure. (Isaiah 46:10,11)

God has put His Words in my mouth and He has covered me in the shadow of His hand. (Isaiah 51:16)

God's Spirit is in me; He has put His words in my mouth. I will only speak His Word. (Isaiah 59:21)

SPEAKING WORDS OF FAITH

I call those things which are not as though they were. (Romans 4:17)

Because I abide in Him and His words abide in me, I ask and it is given unto me. (John 15:7)

God's Word is near me, in my mouth and in my heart; It is the word of faith that I speak. (Romans 10:8)

Faith comes by hearing His Word. As I hear and speak His Word, I increase my faith. (Romans 10:17)

I continue to speak God's Word. I meditate in It day and night; I see and do what He says according to His Word. I make my way prosperous and have good success. (Joshua 1:8)

According to my faith, so be it unto me. (Matthew 9:29)

When I pray, I believe I receive the things I desire. I believe and have no doubt in my heart. Therefore, when I pray (or say) believing what His Word says, I do receive. (Mark 11:23,24)

I ask and it is given to me, I seek and I find, I knock and it is opened unto me, because I ask according to His Word. (Matthew 7:7,8)

I thank You, Lord, that You hasten to perform Your Word in my life. (Jeremiah 1:12)

SPEAKING WORDS OF FAITH

Lord, Your Word is forever settled in heaven. You <u>will</u> <u>not</u> call It back and You continue to perfect that which concerns me. (Psalm 119:89; Isaiah 31:2; Psalm 138:8)

Lord, I know that You can do everything and that no thought can be withheld from You. (Job 42:2)

God gives us the Holy Spirit and works miracles among us by our faith. (Galatians 3:5)

The Lord gives us rest in all that He promises. Not one word of His promises fail. (I Kings 8:56)

Not even one word which the Lord has spoken fails; all come to pass. (Joshua 21:45)

Lord, You bring the counsel of the heathen to nothing, and cause the devices of people to be ineffective. Your counsel stands forever. (Psalm 33:10,11)

Lord, You are faithful; You establish me and guard me from the evil one. (II Thessalonians 3:3)

GRACE-FAVOR

I am what I am by God's grace; His grace was not given to me in vain. (I Corinthians 15:10)

God's grace is sufficient for me. When I am at my weakest, His strength is made perfect. (II Corinthians 12:9)

God makes all grace abound toward me so that I always, at all times and in all ways, have all sufficiency of all things. (II Corinthians 9:8)

I have found grace in God's sight; He knows me by name. (Exodus 33:17)

Jesus increased in wisdom and stature and in favor with God and with man, and so do I. (Luke 2:52)

Mercy and truth are in my heart; I find favor and good understanding in the sight of God and man. (Proverbs 3:3,4)

GRACE-FAVOR

The Lord is my sun and shield; He gives me grace and glory. He withholds no good thing from me, because I walk uprightly. (Psalm 84:11)

I come boldly to Your throne of grace to obtain mercy and find grace to help in my time of need. (Hebrews 4:16)

When I confess my sins, You are faithful to forgive and cleanse me from all unrighteousness. Thank You, Lord for being merciful to me and remembering my iniquities no more. (I John 1:9; Hebrews 8:12)

I thank You, Lord that You are merciful, gracious, full of compassion, and slow to anger. (Psalm 103:8; 145:8)

Lord, your divine favor produces:

Supernatural increase and promotion in my life. (Genesis 41:40)

Total restoration of everything the enemy has stolen. (I Sam 30;18)

Honor in the midst of our adversaries. (Exodus 11:3)

Increased assets, especially in the area of real estate. (Deuteronomy 33:23)

Greater victories in the midst of greater or impossible odds. (Joshua 11:20)

Recognition and promotion by God even when we seem least likely to receive it. (I Samuel 16:22)

Prominence and preferential treatment in every area. (Esther 2:17)

Petitions granted for us even by ungodly authorities. (Esther 5:8)

Policies, rules, regulations, decisions and laws changed or reversed to our advantage. (Esther 8:5)

Battles won in which we won't even have to fight because God fights them for us. (Psalm 44:3)

PEACE

The peace of God, which passes all human understanding, keeps my heart and mind at rest in Christ. (Philippians 4:7)

I am filled with the fruit of the Spirit, which is love, joy, peace, long-suffering, gentleness, goodness, faith, meekness and temperance. (Galatians 5:22,23)

I am spiritually minded, therefore, I have life and peace. (Romans 8:6)

God is not the author of confusion, but of peace. I thank Him that His peace rules in my heart. (I Corinthians 14:33; Colossians 3:15)

The God of peace makes me perfect in every good work to do His will, working in me that which is well-pleasing in His sight, through Jesus. (Hebrews 13:20,21)

Jesus has given me peace; my heart is neither troubled nor afraid, it rests in Him. (John 14:27)

The Lord blesses me with peace. (Psalm 29:11)

I cast all my cares on Christ because He cares for me. I cast all my burdens on Him and He sustains me. He will not allow me to be moved. (I Peter 5:7; Psalm 55:22)

Christ is the Prince of Peace and of His peace there is no end. I am a joint heir with Jesus, so there is no end to my peace either. (Isaiah (9:6,7; Romans 8:17)

The covenant of God's peace will not be removed from me. (Isaiah 54:10)

God is no respecter of persons. He gives glory, honor and peace to me because I obey Him and do His work. (Romans 2:11,10)

I trust You Lord, You are my God. I am in Your hands; You deliver me from my enemies and from those who persecute me. (Psalm 31:14,15)

My ways please the Lord, He makes even my enemies to be at peace with me. (Proverbs 16:7)

When my heart is overwhelmed, I go to the Rock that is higher than I. (Psalm 61:2)

I will be still, Lord and know that you are God. (Psalm 46:10)

SLEEP

I lay down and sleep; the Lord keeps me. (Psalm 3:5)

I lay down in peace and sleep, for You, Lord, keep me in safety. (Psalm 4:8)

He that keeps me neither slumbers nor sleeps. He keeps me from evil. (Psalm 121:4,7)

I am God's beloved and He gives me sleep. (Psalm 127:2)

When I lie down, I am not afraid; my sleep shall be sweet. I will not be afraid of sudden fear for the Lord is my confidence. (Proverbs 3:24-26)

The Lord keeps us. We do not have colic, insomnia, sleep disorders or nightmares. (Psalm 3:5)

God has replenished my weary and sorrowful soul and my sleep is restful. (Jeremiah 31:25,26)

God refreshes me and gives me rest. (Matthew 11:28)

FREEDOM

I continue in His Word; His Word is the truth and that truth sets me free. (John 8:31,32)

Christ has made me free and I remain free. (John 8:36)

I stand fast in the liberty Christ has given me and I will not be caught again in any yoke of bondage. (Galatians 5:1)

The law of the Spirit of life in Christ Jesus has made me free from the law of sin and death. (Romans 8:2)

OBEDIENCE

I obey God's voice; I walk in all His ways as He commands me to and it is well with me. (Jeremiah 7:23)

I stay submitted to God; I resist you, devil and you must flee from me. (James 4:7)

I am willing and obedient and I do eat the good of the land. (Isaiah 1:19)

I have chosen whom I will serve; as for me and my house, we will serve the Lord. (Joshua 24:15)

JOY

God fills me with all joy and peace that I have an abundance of hope, through the power of the Holy Ghost. (Romans 15:13)

Sorrow and sadness flee from me and I have gladness and everlasting joy. (Isaiah 35:10)

He gives me the oil of joy for mourning and praise to replace heaviness. Therefore, I praise Him, with joy, in every situation. (Isaiah 61:3)

The Lord has redeemed me, my mourning is turned into joy. He comforts me and causes me to rejoice instead of sorrow. (Jeremiah 31:11,13)

Jesus' joy is in me and my joy is full. My heart rejoices in Him and no one can take my joy from me. (John 15:11; 16:22)

In Your presence, Lord, is fullness of joy. Your joy is my strength. (Psalm 16:11; Nehemiah 8:10)

The Lord my God is in my midst. The Mighty One saves. He rejoices over me with joy. (Zephaniah 3:17)

Restore to me the joy of Your salvation and uphold me by Your Spirit. I have joy in Your strength, O Lord; in Your salvation I greatly rejoice. (Psalm 51:12; 21:1)

God is my salvation, my strength and my song. Therefore, with joy I draw water from the wells of salvation (victory, health, prosperity, deliverance). (Isaiah 12:2,3)

I will be joyful in glory and sing aloud on my bed. (Psalm 149:5)

STRENGTH

I wait upon You, Lord; I am of good courage and You strengthen my heart. (Psalm 27:14)

The Lord is my strength, my song and my salvation.** (Psalm 118:14) ** Note: The word salvation includes everything we will ever need; salvation, healing, prosperity, deliverance, forgiveness, etc.

I can do all things through Christ Who strengthens me. (Philippians 4:13)

The Lord arms me with strength for every battle. He is my rock, my fortress, my deliverer, my God, my strength; I trust in Him. (Psalm 18:39; 18:2)

Lord, You are my refuge and strength. You are always here to help in time of trouble. (Psalm 46:1)

We sing and praise Your power Lord; You are exalted in Your own strength. (Psalm 21:13)

The Lord saves His own. I am His own. He hears me and saves me with the saving strength of His right hand. (Psalm 20:6)

The Lord is my light and my salvation; He is the strength of my life, whom shall I fear. (Psalm 27:1)

The Lord gives power to me when I am weary; and when I have no power, He increases my strength. (Isaiah 40:29)

I wait upon You, Lord; You renew my strength so I can mount up with wings as eagles, run and not be weary, walk and not faint. (Isaiah 40:31)

Lord, You satisfy my mouth with good things; my youth is renewed like the eagle's. (Psalm 103:5)

The joy of the Lord is my strength. (Nehemiah 8:10)

The Lord is the strength of my life; I do not fear. I am strengthened with all might by His Spirit. (Psalm 27:1; Ephesians 3:16)

The Lord is my strength in time of trouble. I am strengthened with His glorious power and I endure patiently with joy. (Psalm 37:39; Colossians 1:11)

The Lord gives me strength and blesses me with peace. (Psalm 29:11)

STRENGTH

The eyes of the Lord run to and fro throughout the whole earth to show Himself strong in my behalf because my heart is perfect before Him. (II Chronicles 16:9)

The Word says let the weak say, I am strong. I am strong in the Lord and in the power of His might. (Joel 3:10; Ephesians 6:10)

Riches and honor come from You, Lord. You reign over all and in Your hand is power and might. In Your hand it is to make great and to give strength to all. By faith, I receive all that You have for me. (I Chronicles 29:12)

God girds me with strength and makes my way perfect. He makes my feet like hind's feet and causes me to walk upon high places. (Psalm 18:32,33)

I am strong in the Lord and in the power of His might; through my union with Him, I draw my strength. (Ephesians 6:10)

KNOWLEDGE

I am filled with the knowledge of His will in all spiritual wisdom and understanding that I might please Him. I am fruitful in every good work and always increasing in the knowledge of Him. (Colossians 1:9,10)

I have knowledge and skill in learning, wisdom and understanding, even as Daniel had. (Daniel 1:17)

In Christ are all the treasurers of wisdom and knowledge. I am renewed in His knowledge and in His image. (Colossians 2:3; 3:10)

It is evident by my good conversation, that I am a wise person endued with knowledge. (James 3:13)

The fear (reverence) of the Lord is beginning of knowledge. I am growing in grace and in the knowledge of Christ. (Proverbs 1:7; II Peter 3:18)

I believe His commandments, and He teaches me good judgment and knowledge. (Psalm 119:66)

The Lord teaches me knowledge and the understanding of His doctrine, as I continue to grow in Him and study His word. (Isaiah 28:9)

I am rooted and grounded in love and understand the width, length, depth and height of Christ's love which passes knowledge, and I am filled with all the fullness of God. (Ephesians 3:17,19)

SPIRITUAL WISDOM AND UNDERSTANDING

I seek You, Lord; You lead me into understanding all things. (Proverbs 28:5)

I am filled with the knowledge of His will with wisdom and spiritual understanding in every area of my life. (Colossians 1:9)

God gives wisdom to all, liberally and without reproach. When I lack wisdom, I ask for Your wisdom Lord and I believe I receive it. (James 1:5)

I receive God's wisdom from above which is pure, peaceable, gentle and easy to be obeyed; it is full of mercy and good fruits without being partial or hypocritical. (James 3:17)

God gives me the spirit of wisdom and revelation in the knowledge of Him. He has enlightened my eyes to understand and know the hope of His calling and the inheritance I have to His riches in glory. (Ephesians 1:17,18)

I hear Your instruction, Lord. I am wise, I keep the ways of wisdom and I am blessed. (Proverbs 8:32,33)

Lord, You have given me the words of the learned and I know the right word, to speak at the right time to those in need. (Isaiah 50:4)

The Word of Christ dwells in me richly in all wisdom. (Colossians 3:16)

The power and wisdom of God is mine because I am in Christ Jesus. (I Corinthians 1:24)

God has made me righteous, sanctified, wise and redeemed in the Anointed Jesus. (I Corinthians 1:30)

SPIRITUAL MATURITY

Jesus is Lord over all things. I don't have a care, because I cast all my cares upon Him. (Philippians 2:10,11; I Peter 5:7)

Life and death are in the power of my tongue. I refuse to speak anything contrary to the Word. (Proverbs 18:21)

Because I continually hear the Word and faith comes by hearing, my faith continues to grow. I have abundant love for everyone. I am righteous and I do not compromise. (Romans 10:17; Psalm 92:12; II Thessalonians 1:3)

I am not a child tossed to and fro at the enemy's will. I speak the truth in love and grow up into Jesus' likeness in all things. I build up the body of Christ by doing my part, working with others and cooperating in love. (Ephesians 4:14-16)

I grow in the knowledge of God. Grace and peace are multiplied unto me. God's divine power has given me all things pertaining to life and godliness. I receive His promises and walk in them. I am made in His image and likeness. (II Peter 1:2-3)

I hear the Word, believe It and mix It with my faith. I enter into a resting place in the Lord, and trust Him to bring His Word to pass. (Hebrews 4:2,3)

I come boldly to the throne of grace obtaining mercy and finding grace for every need. (Hebrews 4:16)

Though the enemy tries my faith, I bring honor and glory to God by refusing to move from my trust in Him and His Word. (I Peter 1:7)

I am not afraid of bad news, my heart is fixed. I trust in the Lord. My heart is established in His Word. I see my desire of victory and the enemy's defeat because God always causes me to triumph in Christ Jesus. (Psalm 112:7,8; II Corinthians 2:14)

SPIRITUAL MATURITY FOR OTHERS

_____ is a new creature in Christ. Old things have passed away. All things have become new in Him and all things are of God. (II Corinthians 5:17)

_____ presents himself a living sacrifice, holy and acceptable to God. _____ is not conformed to this world but is continually transformed by renewing his mind with the Word. (Romans 12:1,2)

_____ seeks <u>first</u> the kingdom of God and His righteousness; therefore, everything that he needs is added unto him. (Matthew 6:33)

_____ is more than a conqueror in Christ. Nothing can separate him from Jesus his Lord. (Romans 8:37-39)

There is no condemnation to _____ because he is in Christ. He walks after the Spirit, not after the flesh. (Romans 8:1)

_____ walks in the light and is conformed to the image of Jesus. The blood of Jesus Christ cleanses him from all sin. (Romans 8:29; I John 1:7)

The love of God is perfected in _____ because he keeps God's Word. (I John 2:5)

_____ believes that Jesus is the Son of God. His victory to overcome the world comes by faith in the Word, and it's inability to fail. (I John 5:4,5)

_____ is fully persuaded that what God promises He will do. (Romans 4:21)

_____ has received the abundance of grace and the gift of righteousness. He reigns in this life through Christ Jesus. (Romans 5:17)

LIFE

The law of the Spirit of life in Christ Jesus has made me free from the law of sin and death. (Romans 8:2)

You have shown me the ways of life; You fill me with joy in Your presence. (Acts 2;28)

My life is hidden with Christ, in God. (Colossians 3:3)

I have been crucified with Christ yet I still live. Christ lives in me and I live by faith in Christ Jesus. He loves me and gave His own life for me. (Galatians 2:20)

I have the Son, therefore, I have life. (I John 5:12)

I am not concerned about the things of life — what I shall eat or drink, what I shall wear, for there is more to life than these things. I seek first the Kingdom of God and His righteousness and all other things are added to me. (Matthew 6:25,33)

By God's divine power, He has given me all things that pertain to life and godliness through His Word and the knowledge of Him. (II Peter 1:3)

Jesus came that I would have life and life more abundantly. I receive that abundant life in Jesus' name. (John 10:10)

ETERNAL LIFE/SALVATION

Jesus is the Way, the Truth, and the Life. No one comes to the Father, but through Him. (John 14:6)

It is a promise of God that I have life in Christ Jesus. (II Timothy 1:1)

I believe in the Son; I have everlasting life. (John 3:36)

Jesus is the resurrection and the life. (John 11:25)

Because I have accepted Jesus to be the Lord of my life, I will dwell in the house of the Lord forever. (Psalm 23:6)

Because of your love, Lord, You have taken all my sins away and remember them no more. You delivered me from hell. You turned Your back on Jesus as He took my place on that cross. You have given me abundant and eternal life and I praise Your Holy name. (Isaiah 38:18,17,16)

ETERNAL LIFE/SALVATION

Anyone that calls upon the name of the Lord shall be saved. (Romans 10:13)

I believe in my heart and confess with my mouth that Jesus Christ is my Lord and that God raised Him from the dead; my heart believes in His righteousness and my mouth confesses salvation, therefore, I am saved. (Romans 10:9,10)

Sin pays its wages with death; God gives us His gift of eternal life through Jesus. (Romans 6:23)

I am in Christ, a new creation; old things have passed away and all things have become new. (II Corinthians 5:17)

God so loved us that He gave His only begotten Son to die for our sins and whoever believes in Him shall not perish but have everlasting life. I believe in my heart and confess with my mouth that Jesus came to die for my sins and suffer for my healings; therefore, I am saved. (John 3:16; Romans 10:9,10)

Because we are flesh and blood, Jesus became flesh and blood, as the seed of Abraham, to die for us. Through His own death, He destroyed the devil who had the power of death. Jesus delivered us from the bondage of fear of death, as well. (Hebrews 2:15-17)

I have accepted Jesus as my Lord, I am saved and God has removed my unrighteousness, my sins and my iniquities never to remember them again. He made me righteous in Christ, made a covenant with me and put His laws in my mind and heart. He is my Father and I am His child. (Hebrews 8:10,12)

I am sanctified through Jesus Christ who was the sacrifice for all sinners; by that one offering for sin, He has sanctified and made me perfect forever. (Hebrews 10:10,12,14)

Jesus loved us and washed us from our sins with His own blood. He has made us kings and priests unto God, our Father. (Revelation 1:5,6)

God's Word says, believe in the Lord Jesus Christ and you shall be saved and your household. Therefore, I thank You, Father, for the salvation of my household in Jesus' name. (Acts 16:31)

TRUSTING GOD

I trust You at all times, You are my refuge. (Psalm 62:8)

You are my rock, my fortress, my deliverer and my strength; in You, alone, do I trust. (Psalm 18:2)

God's way is perfect. His Word is proven; He is a shield to me because I trust in Him. (II Samuel 22:31)

I trust You, Lord, with all my heart and lean not to my own understanding. (Proverbs 3:5)

I put trust in You, Lord and I do not fear what man can do to me. (Psalm 56:11)

Lord, You are my refuge from the storm; my shade from the heat and You are everlasting strength; I trust in You. (Isaiah 25:4; 26:3,4)

You are the Saviour of all men, I trust You. (I Timothy 4:10)

I trust You, Lord and not in uncertain riches. You give me richly all things to enjoy. (I Timothy 6:17)

I do not trust in myself but in God Who raises the dead. (II Corinthians 1:9)

I draw near to You, Lord; I put my trust in You and I declare all Your works. (Psalm 73:28)

I am not afraid of bad news; my heart is steadfast, trusting You, Lord. (Psalm 112:7)

I trust You, Lord, not in my own strength or my wisdom. I praise Your name for You have saved me from my enemies and have put those who hate me to shame. (Psalm 44:6-8)

I trust You, Lord, and I am as Mount Zion which cannot be removed but abides forever. (Psalm 125:1)

HOPE

When the Word talks about hope, It means to trust or expect with confidence. Hope is the blueprint of your faith. It is the vision of what you have believed for, but do not yet see with your natural eye. Faith is the heavenly, spiritual substance which brings your hope (vision) into being. (Hebrews 11:1)

I hope in You Lord; I am of good courage and You strengthen my heart. I continually hope in You and praise You more and more. (Psalm 31:24; 71:14)

Lord, You are my hiding place and my shield. I hope (trust) in Your Word, and wait for You. (Psalm 119:114; 130:5)

I refuse to be discouraged, or defeated, doubt or fear. My God is a God of hope; I abound in hope through the power of the Holy Ghost and hope makes me never ashamed. (Romans 15:13; 5:5)

When I am discouraged, I hope in God. He is my help; I praise Him. (Psalm 42:11)

Lord, You are my hope in the day of evil; You are my hope in the future. (Jeremiah 17:17; 31:17)

Your eye is upon me for I fear (reverence) You and hope (trust) in Your mercy. You are my help and shield; I wait for You, Lord. (Psalm 33:18,20)

I have confidence in You, Lord, knowing that whatever I ask according to Your Word, You hear; and whatever I ask, I have. (I John 5:14,15)

I am complete in Christ. He is my hope of glory (God's manifest presence in answer to my situation). (Colossians 2:10; 1:27)

Jesus is my Saviour; I am of the house of Jehovah. I hold fast to His Word with confidence and I rejoice in the hope that I have in Him. (Hebrews 3:6)

RIGHTEOUSNESS

I have been recreated in righteousness and true holiness. (Ephesians 4:24)

I am established in righteousness; I am far from oppression. I do not fear; I am far from terror; it does not come near me. (Isaiah 54:14)

My righteousness is of the Lord; my heritage from Him is that no weapon formed against me prospers and every tongue that rises against me is condemned. (Isaiah 54:17)

I am the righteousness of God in Christ because God made Christ to be sin for me. (II Corinthians 5:21)

I do not fear for He is with me; I am not dismayed for He is my God. He strengthens, helps and upholds me with His right hand of righteousness. (Isaiah 41:10)

I am in Christ; I am a new creation; old things have passed away and all things in me have become new in Him. (II Corinthians 5:17)

The eyes of the Lord are upon the righteous and His ears hear their cries. I am righteous, as I cry He hears and delivers me out of all my troubles. (Psalm 34:15,17)

I am righteous and the Lord delivers me out of all afflictions. (Psalm 34:9)

POWER

The Lord gives me strength and power. (Psalm 68:35)

Jesus has given me power to tread upon serpents and scorpions and over all the power of the enemy; nothing shall by any means hurt me. (Luke 10:19)

I am strong in the Lord and in the power of His might. (Ephesians 6:10)

God's Word, in my mouth, is alive and full of power, sharper than any two edged sword. (Hebrews 4:12)

By God's divine power, He has given me all things pertaining to life and godliness. (II Peter 1:3)

Because I believe in the Lord and am baptized in the Holy Spirit these signs follow me; in His name I cast out devils, speak with new tongues, lay hands on the sick and they do recover; should I take up any deadly serpent or drink any deadly thing, it will not harm me. (Mark 16:17,18)

My faith is not in the wisdom of men but in God's power. (I Corinthians 2:5)

God continues to reveal to me the greatness of His power that is unending and without measure. His power is above all principalities, powers, mights and dominions, above every name in this world and the one to come. That power is in me because I an His child. (Ephesians 1:19-22)

God has not given me the spirit of fear, but of power and of love and of a sound mind. (II Timothy 1:7)

God is able and does exceedingly abundantly above all that I ask or think according to His power that works in me. (Ephesians 3:20)

HEALTH AND HEALING

Every disease germ, virus, bacteria, fungus, infection or parasite that touches my body dies instantly in Jesus' name. Because Jesus Himself took my infirmities and sicknesses, I forbid any lying wonder, symptom, imbalance, sickness, disease, weakness, infirmity, malfunction, abnormality, imperfection, infection, defect, deficiency, deformity, pain, irregularity, immune deficiency, allergy, growth, tumor or cyst of any kind in or on my body. I take authority over my body and command every cell, tissue, bone, nerve, joint, fiber, muscle, organ, fluid, every part of my blood, teeth, hair, skin, nails and every system, individually and collectively, to function perfectly, as God created it to function, in Jesus' name. (Matthew 8:17; I Peter 2:24; Psalm 34:20; Proverbs 20:12; II Samuel 14:25; Acts 3:7; Psalm 139:14; Romans 4:17; Genesis 1:27

We hold fast the profession of our faith without wavering; for He is faithful that promised. Our healing (wholeness and soundness) is guaranteed in Jesus's name. (Hebrews 10:23; I Peter 2:24; Hebrews 7:22)

I praise God!! I have faith knowing that as I trust in Him and His Word, He will not make me ashamed. My healing is complete. (Romans 10:11)

The affliction of _____ will not come again a second time. God has made a complete end of _____ in _____. (Nahum 1:9)

The Lord is good; a stronghold in the day of trouble. He knows that I trust Him. He has made an utter end and no affliction or addiction will come again. (Nahum 1:7-9)

I wait on the Lord; I keep His way. He exalts me; the wicked are cut off and I see it. I saw the wicked in great power, spreading himself as a green bay tree (growing from itself, like cancer), he passed away and is not. They looked for him, but could not find him. The end of the wicked is cut off. The Lord helps, saves and delivers me because I trust in Him. (Psalm 37:34-36,38,40)

I am redeemed from the curse of the law according to Galatians 3:13. In the name of Jesus I refuse to allow sickness or disease in this body. (Galatians 3:13; Job 22:28)

HEALTH AND HEALING

God calls heaven and earth to witness this day that He has set before me life and death, blessing and cursing. I choose life that both I and my seed will live to love the Lord, obey His voice and cling to Him. He is our life and the length of our days; we dwell in the land which the Lord has given us. (Deuteronomy 30:19.20)

I pay close attention to God's Word; I listen to what He says. I keep reading His Word and keep It in the midst of my heart because His Words are life and health to my body. (Proverbs 4:20-22)

Surely He hath borne my griefs (sicknesses) and carried my sorrows (diseases). (Isaiah 53:4)

He was wounded for my transgressions (sins), He was bruised (striped, beaten) for my iniquities (sin, guilt), the chastisement (correction) of my peace (well-being) was upon Him; and with His stripes I am healed. (Isaiah 53:5)

I bless You, Lord, I forget not all Your benefits; You forgive all my iniquities and You heal all my diseases. You redeem my life from all destruction. (Psalm 103:2-4)

I serve the Lord my God, and He blesses my bread and my water; He takes sickness away from the midst of me. There is nothing barren in my land and the number of my days He will fulfill. (Exodus 23:25,26)

Oh Lord, I cry unto You, and You heal me. (Psalm 30:2)

I do not fear, I believe and I am made whole. (Luke 8:50)

I call upon the Lord and He saves, heals, delivers and sets me free. (Psalm 55:16)

Your mercy is upon me as I hope in You, Lord. My hope is in Your mercy. You deliver me from death, You keep me alive in famine. You are my shield. My heart rejoices in You and I trust in Your holy name. (Psalm 33:22, 18-21)

The Lord has spoken and it is done; He has commanded and it stands fast. With His stripes I am healed. (Psalm 33:9; Isaiah 53:5)

I am righteous and the Lord delivers me out of all afflictions. (Psalm 34:19)

HEALTH AND HEALING

No harm comes near me, no evil befalls me and no plague or calamity comes near my dwelling. He gives His angels charge over me to keep me in all ways. (Psalm 91:10,11)

He sent His Word and healed me and delivered me from all destructions. (Psalm 107:20)

No weapon, including sickness, disease, infection, pain, infirmity or weakness, formed against me shall prosper. (Isaiah 54:17)

God hastens to carry out His Word on my behalf. I am redeemed from sickness. (Jeremiah 1:12)

No good thing which the Lord has spoken fails; all come to pass. I am healed. (Joshua 21:45)

Lord, Your eyes are on me because I am righteous. Your ears hear my cries. You hear and deliver me out of all my troubles; I trust in You so I am not desolate. (Psalm 34:15,17,22)

I praise You, Lord, for Your goodness and for Your wonderful works toward me. (Psalm 107:21)

Sickness and disease are part of the curse of the law, but according to Galatians 3:13, Christ has redeemed me from the curse of the law, being made a curse for me. (Deuteronomy 28: Galatians 3:13)

I keep the commandments of the Lord and He takes <u>all</u> sickness away from me and does not allow any disease to come upon me. (Deuteronomy 7:12,15)

The Lord preserves and keeps _____ alive; _____ is blessed upon the earth, and You, Lord, strengthen and heal _____. (Psalm 41:2,3)

You have heard my prayers, seen my tears and You, Lord, have healed _____. (II Kings 20:5)

The covenant of the Lord stands forever and the thoughts of His heart are to all generations. He took an oath and cannot lie. Therefore, according to the covenant, I am healed. (Judges 2:1; Psalm 33:11; Hebrews 6:17,18)

Body, I am speaking to you in Jesus' name. Sickness, pain, infirmity, disease and weakness have no part in you. You have been set free and you <u>will</u> remain free. Every part of you (from the top of your head to the soles of your feet) functions perfectly. (John 8:36; Job 22:28)

BONES

My bones are moistened with marrow, free from cancer, leukemia, arthritis, brittleness and all disease. (Job 21:24)

I am righteous. The Lord keeps all my bones and not one of them is broken. (Psalm 34:20)

Bones, you are as strong as pieces of brass and bars of iron. (Job 40:18)

The Word is health to my flesh and strength to my bones. (Proverbs 4:22)

SKIN

There is no blemish on my body from the top of my head to the soles of my feet. There is no skin cancer, skin disease, burns, warts, cysts, acne, allergy, eczema, tumor or growth. (II Samuel 14:25)

HAIR

Many times during the treatment of disease, a person will lose his hair. It is most helpful, if you use the Word to come against this loss before it begins. Also, by building your faith in the Word, you do not need to lose your hair as you get older.

The very hairs on my head are numbered. Every day God replaces those I lose with new healthy hair. (Luke 12:7)

My hair is in abundance, even as Absalom's was. I refuse to receive thinning hair or baldness in Jesus' name. (II Samuel 14:26)

FEET

My feet, like those of the Israelites, do not swell. (Nehemiah 9:21)

I walk before the Lord and He keeps my feet from falling. The Lord lifts me up and strengthens my feet and ankle bones. (Acts 3:7; Psalm 116:8)

Lord, You set my feet upon a rock and establish my steps. (Psalm 40:2)

You make my feet like the feet of a deer; You enlarge my path so my feet do not slip. (Psalm 18:33,36)

Every place my feet walk, the Lord has given to me. (Joshua 1:3)

BLOOD

In the name of Jesus, my blood is healthy and flows freely throughout my body with no cholesterol buildup, free of all disease, infection, anemia, excessive or abnormal blood clots or blockages of any kind in any vein or artery. There is no lupus, leukemia, immune deficiency. In Jesus' name, my liver and both kidneys function perfectly without fail. They perform every service God created them to do. My blood pressure is perfect. There are no strokes, heart problems or heart attacks. (Job 22:28)

EYES AND EARS

My eyes see perfectly and do not grow dim; my ears hear perfectly and listen well. (Isaiah 32:3)

The Word says the deaf hear and the blind see, so my ears and eyes function perfectly. (Isaiah 42:18)

I receive the hearing ears and the seeing eyes which the Lord has made. Hearing loss, infections, deafness, blindness, glaucoma and cataracts have no place in me. (Proverbs 20:12; Job 22:28)

I am called by God's name. He created me for His glory; He formed me. He made me perfect in every way, including perfect eyesight and hearing. (Isaiah 43:7)

My ears hear others speaking the wonderful works of God. (Acts 2:11)

My eyes see and my ears hear. I am blessed. (Matthew 13:16)

I am blessed because I hear the Word of God and keep it! (Luke 11:28)

The Lord God has opened my ears. (Isaiah 50:5)

TEETH

My mouth has no infections, cancer, gum or bone disease and is large enough for all my teeth. My gums are perfect and healthy. My teeth are white, straight, strong and perfect and have no cavities. Fillings, braces, extractions, root canals, caps, crowns, bridges and dentures are unnecessary. Each tooth comes up in its proper place and straight. I have no problems with wisdom teeth. (Job 22:28)

HEALTH AND HEALING PRAYER

Lord, I thank You that every part of each of us is written in Your Book. Each member of our family is perfectly formed for You, Lord create only good and perfect things. Our eyes see perfectly and our ears hear perfectly for that is how You created them. We are healthy and whole from the top of our heads to the soles of our feet. I command every system, (digestive, nervous, reproductive, immune, respiratory and circulatory) and all of its parts, individually and collectively to function perfectly in Jesus's name. I speak to every organ, muscle, tissue, ligament, tendon, joint, cartilage, fiber, bone, marrow, nerve, cell, gland, artery, vein, capillary, platelet, white and red blood cell, plasma, hemoglobin, skin, spinal cord and brain and I command everything to line up with the Word and function perfectly. Every organ and system is fully developed and functions perfectly. There is no imperfection, abnormality, infection, defect, deficiency, deformity, irregularity, malfunction, allergy, growth, tumor, cyst, weakness, imbalance, pain, infirmity or lying sign or wonder in this body, in Jesus' name.

HURT, HARM AND ATTACK OF ENEMY

Sickness and disease keep us in bondage to the enemy through how we feel and what we see and hear from the doctor. There is fear of what the doctor says, instead of faith in what the Lord says. In cases involving children, there is fear of what the authorities, social services, etc. will say and do. AIDS, cancer, different growths, malignancies, fear, destruction, radiation, chemotherapy, surgery, fear of authorities and evil reports by doctors and others are fiery darts sent by the enemy. Many times, especially where children are concerned, there is no choice but to consent to surgery and/or treatment. It is extremely important to put forth the Word day and night. Claim the following Scriptures along with others the Lord shows you. Remember, our bodies, respond to THE WORD!! Your situation can be changed by THE WORD!!

(The following Scriptures may also be used for individuals, businesses and ministries under attack by forces of darkness through persecution, addition and debt.)

No manner of hurt is found in _____ because I believe in my God. He is true to His Word. (Daniel 6:23)

HURT, HARM AND ATTACK OF ENEMY

God delivers and rescues _____. He works signs and wonders in heaven and earth. He has delivered _____ from the power of the lions (satan and demon spirits that destroy). (Daniel 6:27)

My God whom I serve is well able to and does deliver _____ from the lions. (Daniel 6:20)

I am not afraid; I speak God's Word for He is with me. No person is able to hurt _____ in Jesus' name. (Acts 18:9,10)

God restores health, wholeness, soundness, and prosperity unto _____ and heals _____ completely. (Jeremiah 30:17)

As _____ drinks any deadly thing*, it shall not hurt him. (Mark 16:18) (* may be applied to any drug put into the body)

NO destruction comes near _____, because I trust completely in my God. (Psalm 91:7)

Sickness and disease, poverty and lack, debt, destruction and death are all the works of the devil and Jesus was manifested to destroy all his works. Therefore, they are destroyed in every area of my life. (I John 3:8)

Nothing shall by any means hurt _____. (Luke 10:19)

God delivers _____ out of all trouble. We see His desire upon our enemies; they are defeated. (Psalm 54:7)

God has delivered _____ in peace from the battle that was against him. (Psalm 55:18)

No weapon formed against _____ shall prosper. (Isaiah 54:17)

The Lord redeems my soul because I am His servant. (Psalm 34:22)

Those who seek to destroy me are confused and put to shame. Those who want to hurt me are turned back in defeat. Those who persecute me are stopped. (Psalm 35:4,3)

Lord, Your eyes are on us because we are righteous, Your ears hear our cries, and You deliver us out of all our troubles. We shall not be desolate because none that trust in You shall ever be desolate. We trust in You. (Psalm 34:15,17,22)

The Lord has heard our prayers, seen our tears and He has healed _____. (II Kings 20:5)

HURT, HARM AND ATTACK OF ENEMY

The Lord speaks and it is done; He commands and it stands fast, therefore no weapon formed against us prospers. (Psalm 33:9; Isaiah 54:17)

Because we are righteous, God keeps all our bones; not one of them shall be broken. (Psalm 34:20)

The Lord takes <u>ALL</u> sickness away from us and will not allow any evil disease upon us. (Deuteronomy 7:15)

I bless You, Lord; I forget not all Your benefits. You forgive all our iniquities, heal all our diseases and redeem us from all destruction. (Psalm 103:1-4)

_____ shall not die but live and declare the works of the Lord. (Psalm 118:17)

I call upon God and He saves me. (Psalm 55:16)

Lord, You satisfy us with Your mercy in manifesting _____'s healing and deliverance. We rejoice and are glad. (Psalm 90:14)

We wait on the Lord and keep His way. He exalts us; the wicked are cut off and we see it. We have seen the wicked in great power spreading himself as a green bay tree (growing from itself as cancer), yet he passed away and <u>IS NOT</u>. We looked for him but could not find him, the end of the wicked is cut off: the Lord helps, saves and delivers us because we trust Him. (Psalm 37:34-36,38,40)

The Lord is good, a stronghold in the day of trouble. He knows that I trust completely in Him; He has made an utter end and that affliction will not come again a second time. (Nahum 1:7-9)

We praise God; we have faith in His Word. We trust in His Word. He will not make us ashamed. (Hebrews 11;6; Romans 10:11)

God sent His Word, heals _____ and delivers him from <u>all</u> destruction. (Psalm 107:20)

We serve the Lord our God and He blesses our bread and water. He takes sickness away from the midst of us. (Exodus 23:25)

The Lord delivers us in the day of trouble. The Lord preserves and keeps _____ alive. We are blessed upon the earth. The Lord strengthens and heals us. (Psalm 41:2,3)

HURT, HARM AND ATTACK OF ENEMY

God creates the fruit of my lips and He heals _____. (Isaiah 57:19)

I and the children God has given me are for signs and wonders. We put our trust in Him; we declare His name and sing praises unto Him. Through His own death, He has destroyed the devil who had the power of death. (Isaiah 8:18; Hebrews 2:12-14)

Satan, you and your works are under our feet. Jesus has bruised (crushed completely, tread upon, shattered and broken in pieces) you and your works. (Romans 16:20)

Our God is a prayer answering, covenant keeping, signs and wonders, miracle working God. (The Entire Bible)

Any affliction or addiction that has attacked me or my seed will not come again. (Nahum 1;9)

No child in this family shall die and none of us shall die before our time. The Lord promises us old age. We shall build houses and live in them, plant trees and fields and eat the fruit of them. (Isaiah 65:20,21)

The God of peace sanctifies us wholly (completely). Our whole spirit, soul (mind) and body is preserved, blameless, complete, undamaged and in tact. (I Thessalonians 5:23)

DRUGS, ALCOHOL AND NICOTINE

(These scriptures can be used for any addiction.)

I refuse to take drugs, drink alcohol or smoke. My body is the temple of the Holy Spirit and it is dedicated to God. I will not allow anything (drugs, alcohol, nicotine, etc.) to defile this temple which is holy unto Him. (I Corinthians 3:16,17)

I glorify God in my spirit and in my body. I refuse to allow anything (drugs, alcohol, nicotine, etc.) in me that would not please Him. (I Corinthians 6:19,20)

I refuse to allow drugs, alcohol or nicotine any place in my life. I give my body to God as a living sacrifice, holy unto Him. (Romans 12:1)

I do not take drugs, drink alcohol, smoke or do anything else that could cause someone to be made weak, become offended or stumble in their walk with the Lord. (Romans 14:21)

I can do all things through Christ. In Jesus' name, I break this habit of _____ because He is my strength. (Philippians 4:13)

God has delivered me from all the powers of darkness including drugs, alcohol and nicotine and has placed me in the kingdom of His Son, Jesus. (Colossians 1:13)

I have come out from, separated myself and do not touch unclean things (drugs, alcohol, nicotine, etc.) for I am God's child. (II Corinthians 6:17,18)

Curse of addiction, I speak to you now, in the name of Jesus. I break your power with the blood of Jesus and the power of His name. You have no place in my life. I forbid you from attacking me or anyone else in my family in Jesus' name now or in generations to come. (Luke 10:19)

I have no fellowship with the unfruitful works of darkness including drugs, alcohol and nicotine. I keep myself from everything that appears to be evil and I hold fast to the good things of the Lord. (Ephesians 5:11; I Thessalonians 5:21,22)

I refuse alcohol of any kind. It is written, no drunkards shall inherit the kingdom of God. (I Corinthians 6:10)

I refuse to give alcohol to anyone because this is not pleasing to God and He will hold me accountable. (Habakkuk 2:15)

DRUGS, ALCOHOL AND NICOTINE

I am not deceived because I receive the wisdom of God which says wine is a mocker and strong drink makes one rage. (Proverbs 20:1)

All the old things (drugs, alcohol and nicotine) I used to do have passed away because I am now a new creation in Christ. All things about me are new in Him. (II Corinthians 5:17)

I submit myself totally and completely to God. I resist you satan and I refuse drugs, alcohol and nicotine. (James 4:7)

Jesus has set me free from drugs, alcohol and nicotine and I remain free in Him. (John 8:36)

Wine and strong drink cause men to make mistakes, see wrongly and stumble in good judgment. I will not drink anything with alcohol in it. (Isaiah 28:7)

I do not love the things of the world (drugs, alcohol and nicotine) because I have the love of the Father in me and I want to please Him. (I John 2:15)

WEIGHT LOSS-DIETING

I can do all things through Christ, Who strengthens me. Lord, give me the strength to lose this weight. (Philippians 4:13)

Lord, I consider Your Word more important for my body than natural food; therefore, when I am not hungry but am tempted to eat, I will concentrate on Your Word instead. (Job 23:12)

Lord, You have made me more than a conqueror in Christ; I can conquer losing this weight in Jesus' name. (Romans 8:37)

Lord, help me daily to lay aside this weight and the sin of gluttony that could easily overwhelm me. I look to You to help me lose each pound, and I praise You for each one I lose. Help me continue to lose weight until I have reached the weight I should be. (Hebrews 12:1)

When I sit down to eat, I diligently consider the food that is before me. I refuse to overeat. I eat only the proper amounts of those foods that are good for me. (Proverbs 23:1)

Lord, I delight myself in You; You give me the desires of my heart. I desire to lose weight and be a testimony to You. (Psalm 37:4)

I declare and establish that I am the perfect height, weight and proportion God would have me to be. (Job 22:28)

I declare and establish that there is no bulimia, anorexia or obesity in my family, in Jesus' name. (Job 22:28)

Body, I am speaking to you, you do nothing that displeases the Lord. You lead a controlled life in every area. You are the perfect weight God wants you to be. You are a temple of the Holy Spirit and a glorious testimony to the Lord. (Job 22:28)

FEAR

The Lord is my light and my salvation; I do not fear. (Psalm 27:1)

God has not given me the spirit of fear, but of power and of love and of a sound mind. (II Timothy 1:7)

God's perfect love casts out fear. God is with me and I do not fear. (I John 4:18; Genesis 26:24)

I refuse to fear, for fear has torment. (I John 4:18)

I have put my trust in God and I do not fear what man can do to me. The Lord is on my side and He is my helper. (Psalm 56:4; Hebrews 13:6)

I am not afraid of sudden fear when it comes, for the Lord is my confidence and He keeps my foot from being taken. (Proverbs 3:25,26)

I am strong; I do not fear, for God comes with vengeance. He repays and He saves me. (Isaiah 35:4)

I am not dismayed for The Lord is my God; He strengthens and helps me. I do not fear for He is with me. God upholds me with the right hand of His righteousness. (Isaiah 41:10)

I do not fear for He has redeemed me; He calls me by name. I am His. (Isaiah 43:1)

I do not fear the reproach of men and I am not afraid of their words and abuse. (Isaiah 51:7)

I am not afraid of any terrors of night (the thoughts of abduction, rape, robbery, the darkness or the things that could happen at night); nor do I fear any sickness or disease for I trust in the Lord my God and He delivers me. (Psalm 91:5,6,2)

STAYING OUT OF STRIFE

A fire goes out when there is no wood. Strife stops with me because I do not carry tales. (Proverbs 26:20)

Because my ways please the Lord, He makes my enemies to be at peace with me. (Proverbs 16:7)

I refuse to speak any corrupt (wrong) words; I speak only words that edify and build up others. My words minister grace to those who hear them. (Ephesians 4:29)

I do not grieve the Holy Spirit because I put all bitterness, wrath, anger, noise, evil speaking and malice far from me. (Ephesians 4:30,31)

A tale bearer reveals secrets: I am of a faithful spirit and conceal them. (Proverbs 11:13)

I control my tongue, therefore, I don't deceive my heart and my religion is not useless but life changing. (James 1:26)

I continually think about and speak things that are true, honest, just, pure, lovely, of good report, virtuous and praise worthy. (Philippians 4:8)

I am a servant of the Lord. I am gentle, ready to teach, patient and meek to everyone. I do not strive. (II Timothy 2:24)

I refuse to speak wrong words because a city (home, family, business, school, church, government) is overthrown by wrong words but is exalted by the blessings of those who are upright before God. (Proverbs 11:11)

I set my will that my mouth speaks no wrong thing. I speak only those things I desire to come to pass. (Psalm 17:3; Job 22:28)

I refuse to yield to a critical spirit, judging or criticizing anyone. I pray for them and let God have His perfect Way in their life. (Ephesians 4:29)

LOVE

I abide in the light (Jesus), I love my brothers and sisters in Christ. I love my neighbor as myself and I serve others.(I John 2:10; Galatians 5:14,13)

I speak the Word in love and I grow up into the Lord Jesus Christ, in all things. (Ephesians 4:15)

I am an imitator of God and as His child, I walk in love as Jesus did. (Ephesians 5:1,2)

The love of God abides in me and fills up my entire being. I forgive and walk in love; I keep His Word, therefore, I give no place to the devil. (John 14:23; Ephesians 4:27)

I walk in love and my ways please the Lord. He makes even my enemies to be at peace with me. (Proverbs 16:7)

The fruit of my spirit is love, joy, peace, longsuffering, gentleness, goodness, faith, meekness and temperance. (Galatians 5:22,23)

The love of God is shed abroad in my heart by the Holy Ghost. I love my enemies. I bless those that curse me. I do good to those that hate me and I pray for those who despitefully use and persecute me. (Romans 5:5; Matthew 5:44)

My love abounds more and more in knowledge and in all judgment. I approve things that are excellent. I am sincere and without offense until the day of Christ and I am filled with the fruits of righteousness. (Philippians 1:9-11)

Everywhere I go, I walk in the life, light and love of You, Lord. (Deuteronomy 30:20; I John 1;5; 4:16)

I endure long and am patient and kind. I do not envy. I do not push myself ahead of others; I am not proud and do not behave rudely or unmannerly. I do not seek my own rights or way; I am not easily offended. I think no evil and I pay no attention to any evil said or done to me. I am not happy at iniquity but I rejoice in the truth. I bear all things, believe all things, hope all things and endure all things. I never fail, because love never fails. (I Corinthians 13:4-8)

I follow after love and desire spiritual gifts; I let all my work be done in love. (I Corinthians 14:1; 16:14)

LOVE

I walk in love. I keep Your Word, Lord and Your love is perfected in me. (I John 2:5; 4:12)

I know and believe God's great love for me. He dwells in me and His love has dominion in every area of my life. (I John 4:16)

I love God and keep His commandments. (I John 5:2)

Christ lives in my heart by faith. I am rooted and grounded in love and I understand the great, all encompassing love of Christ. I am filled with all the fullness of God. (Ephesians 3:16,19)

God is able to do exceedingly abundantly above all I ask or think because His power works in me. (Ephesians 3:20)

I walk humbly, meekly and patiently, holding up others in love. (Ephesians 4:1,2)

FOR A MATE

I read in Your Word, Lord, that I will not fail nor lack a mate. I am fully persuaded that You perform that which You have promised. (Isaiah 34:16; Romans 4:21)

Lord, You help me; I am not confused. I have set my face like a flint and I know I will not be disappointed! (Isaiah 50:7)

You perfect that which concerns me for I delight myself in You, Lord and You give me the desires of my heart, including my perfect mate. (Psalm 138:8; 37:4)

You delight in me and I will be married. Lord, You, rejoice over me, as the bridegroom rejoices over the bride. (Isaiah 62:4,5)

I know there is a time for every matter and every work under heaven and You make all things beautiful in Your time. (Ecclesiastes 3:17,11)

Two are better than one. For when one falls the other will lift him up. Christ, my mate and I are a three-fold cord and we are not easily broken. (Ecclesiastes 4:9-12)

Father, Your Word says, a man who finds a wife finds a good thing and receives Your favor. I thank You, Lord, for that favor operating in my life. (Proverbs 18:22)

Every man should have his own wife and every woman should have her own husband. According to Your Word, Lord, so be it unto me. (I Corinthians 7:2; Luke 1:38)

FOR A MATE

I thank You, Father, that my husband will love me as Christ loved the church and gave Himself for it. (Ephesians 5:25)

It is not good that man should be alone, so Lord, I trust You to supply me with a help-mate. (Genesis 2:18)

I thank You, Lord, because You bring upon me all the good You have promised me. I thank You for my mate. (Jeremiah 32:42)

I will love my mate as much as I love myself. (Ephesians 5:28)

I will leave my mother and father, and be joined with my mate, the two of us shall be as one. (Ephesians 5:31)

MARRIAGE

We set our wills to walk in God's agapé love! We endure long, we are patient and kind. Neither of us is envious nor jealous; we trust each other completely. We do not boast, nor desire self glory. We are not proud. We are never rude, unmannerly, or unkind to each other or anyone else. Neither of us insists on having his own way, but yields to the needs and desires of the other! We are not easily offended, touchy or resentful; instead, we are patient, loving and kind. We overlook each other's faults and shortcomings. We do not hold them against one another knowing love covers everything. We are truthful with each other at all times. We stand together in hard times bearing each other up. We work together and not against each other. We always look for and believe the best in each other and our children. Together, we endure everything that comes along, because the love we have for each other is God's agapé love and it can never fail. (I Corinthians 13:4-8)

We have left our parents, are joined to each other and have become one. We are as one body. (Genesis 2:24)

My wife is my companion and the wife of my covenant. I will not deal wrongly with her nor she with me. God has made us one. Our seed is Godly seed. (Malachi 2:14,15)

We have been joined together before God and no man shall separate us or tear us apart. (Mark 10:9)

Together, we are better than one. When one falls, the other lifts him up. Christ, my spouse and I make three-fold cord that is not easily broken. (Ecclesiastes 4:9-12)

We delight ourselves in You, Lord. You give us the desires of our hearts and Your perfect all things that concern us. (Psalm 37:4; 138:8)

We have become one; the love of God has been poured into our hearts by the Holy Spirit. (Genesis 2:24; Romans 5:5)

God instructs, teaches and guides us by His Holy Spirit in every area of our marriage. (Psalm 32:8)

Our marriage grows stronger every day because it is based on Your Word, Lord. We are rooted and grounded in Your love. (Ephesians 3:17)

We are of one mind, compassionate, loving and courteous toward one another. We respect each other and dwell in peace, therefore, our prayers are not hindered in any way. (I Peter 3:8,7)

BARRENNESS AND MISCARRIAGE

I will not miscarry nor be barren. Lord, You will see to it that I carry this child to its full term. (Exodus 23:26)

We are obedient to the covenant. The Lord blesses us. He loves and blesses the fruit of my womb. Neither we nor our seed shall be barren. (Deuteronomy 7:12-14)

God has formed this child in my womb. He knows and has sanctified him. (Jeremiah 1:5)

My baby will be delivered in God's time. (Luke 2:6)

Blessed is the fruit of my body (my children). (Deuteronomy 28:4)

The Lord blesses all that we set our hand to. We set our hand to raising our children for His honor and glory. (Deuteronomy 28:8)

As the Lord makes the barren woman to keep house and to be a joyful mother of children, so am I. (Psalm 113:9)

As the Lord opened Sarah's womb and she conceived and bore a child, so shall I in Jesus' name. (Genesis 11:30; 17:16,19)

PREGNANCY

**These scriptures may be said over adopted or foster children as well.

I am highly favored for You are with me, Lord. I am blessed among women and blessed is the fruit of my womb. (Luke 1:28,42)

**My child increases in wisdom, stature and in favor with God and man, even as Jesus did. (Luke 2:52)

I will not miscarry nor be barren. Lord, You will see to it that I carry this child to its full term. (Exodus 23:26)

I have been redeemed from the curse. I will have a problem free pregnancy and a safe, quick, easy and natural delivery, free from complications. (Genesis 3:16; Galatians 3:13; Job 22:28)

We are obedient to the covenant. The Lord blesses us above all people. He loves us and blesses the fruit of my womb. Neither we nor our seed shall be barren. (Deuteronomy 7:12-14)

**Father, I praise You because You give only good and perfect gifts. You have given us this child, so we know he is good and perfect in every way — spirit, soul and body. (James 1:17)

PREGNANCY

**Lord, I praise You that Your Word does not return to You void. It accomplishes that which You please and It prospers in the things whereunto It is sent. You honor You Word above Your Name and You watch over Your Word to perform It. I put this child into Your hands, knowing that You perfect all things that concern us! Now Lord, be it unto us according to Your Word! (Isaiah 55:11; Psalm 138:2; Jeremiah 1:12; Psalm 138:8; Luke 1:38)

**I prayed for this child and You, Lord, have given what I asked for. I dedicate him to You; as long as he lives, he shall serve You. (I Samuel 1:27,28)

**I, and the children You have given me, are for signs and wonders. All of my children are taught of You, Lord and great is their peace. (Isaiah 8:18;54:13)

Before I even labor, I deliver and before any pain, my child is born. (Isaiah 66:7)

Lord, I thank You that every part of this baby is written in Your Book. This child is perfectly formed for You, Lord, create the seeing eye and the hearing ear. He is healthy and whole from the top of his head to the soles of his feet. I command every system (digestive, immune, nervous, skeletal, urinary, endocrine, reproductive, respiratory, circulatory), every organ, muscle, tissue, bone, fiber, nerve, cell, marrow, joint, tendon, ligament, artery, vein, capillary, brain and blood cell to line up with Your Word. I forbid any malfunction, deformity, defect, deficiency, imperfection, infection, irregularity, abnormality, allergy, growth, tumor, cyst, weakness, imbalance, symptom, pain, infirmity or lying wonder in my child's body in the name of Jesus. Every disease germ, virus, sickness, fungus, infection or parasite that touches this baby's body dies instantly, because Your Word says we have been redeemed from the curse of the law. Your Word says, let the redeemed of the Lord says so and we do in Jesus' name. (Psalm 139:16; Proverbs 20:12; Galatians 3:13)

**Our child will obey us in the Lord, for this is right. He will honor us because this is the first commandment with promise. It is well with him and he will live a long, happy, healthy, successful, prosperous, blessed life upon the earth. (Ephesians 6:1-3)

PREGNANCY

**Lord, we rejoice in the miracle of this child and we delight ourselves in You. We thank You that this child will be to us all that our hearts desire. We set our wills to raise him in the nurture and admonition of You, Lord. (Psalm 37:4; Ephesians 6:4)

**This child is called by God's name. He has created him for His glory, He has formed him, He has made him. (Isaiah 43:7)

CHILDREN

Father, You say in Your Word that, concerning the works of Your hand, we are to command You. (Isaiah 45:11) So, according to Your Word, I command my children to be:

Perfect — in every way — spirit, soul and body. You give us only good and perfect gifts. You have given us these children, so I know they are good and perfect. (James 1:17)

Wise — Wise for they hear their father's instruction and they obey. They seek You from an early age and do what is right. (Proverbs 13:1; II Corinthians 34:3)

Prosperous and Successful — They continually speak Your Word; they meditate on It day and night; they observe and do all that Your Word tells them to. They prosper and succeed. (Joshua 1:8)

Talented — You have given them their talents and You bless everything they set their hands to. They are blessed in scholastics, relationships, athletics, music, ministries, businesses, finances andlife. Their talents and abilities are for Your honor and glory. (Deuteronomy 28:8; Job 22:28)

Strong — You have given them strength and bless them with peace. (Psalm 29:11)

Healthy — Because You have fearfully and wonderfully made them, sickness, disease, infection, illness, weakness, pain, infirmity symptoms, lying wonders and other satanic manifestations or attacks have no place in them in Jesus' name. (Psalm 139:14)

Confident — They have faith in You; knowing that You perfect all things that concern them. They have confidence in themselves that they can do all things through Christ. (Philippians 1:6; 4:13)

Intelligent — They have the mind of Christ and knowledge and skill in learning. (I Corinthians 2:16, Daniel 1:17)

Respectful and Obedient — They respect others, honor their fathers and mothers; it is well with them. They have long life. (Ephesians 6:1-3)

CHILDREN

My children are taught of You, Lord and great is their peace. We are established in righteousness; we are far from oppression, and we do not fear. Terror does not come near us. No weapon formed against us prospers and every tongue that rises against us, we condemn. (Isaiah 54:13,14,17)

My children are my heritage from You, Lord; the fruit of my womb is Your reward to me. (Psalm 127:3)

My children are wise and keep Your law, Lord. They honor and obey me in all things for this is well pleasing unto You. (Proverbs 28:7; Colossians 3:20)

I bring up my children in the nurture and admonition of You, Lord. I provoke them unto love and to good works. (Ephesians 6:4; Hebrews 10:24)

My children are trained according to the Word of God, even when they are older they <u>will</u> not depart from It. They will be lenders and not borrowers. (Proverbs 22:6,7)

God pours His Spirit upon my children and His blessing is upon them. I and the children God has given me are for signs and wonders. (Isaiah 44:3; 8:18)

My children honor their father and mother and it is well with them. Their days are long upon the earth. (Ephesians 6:1-3)

God contends with those who contend with me. He saves, heals, prospers and delivers my children. (Isaiah 49:25)

Thank You, Lord for giving my children perfect hearts, to keep Your commandments, Your testimonies, Your laws and to do all that You have for them to do. (I Chronicles 29:19)

Because I hearken diligently to the voice of God, to observe and do as He commands, His blessings come upon me and all that I set my hand to. I set my hand to my children knowing and serving the Lord and they do in Jesus' name. (Deuteronomy 28:8)

My children continue in You, Lord, and their seed is established before You. (Psalm 102:28)

I did not labor in vain nor bring forth my children for trouble. They and their children are my seed and we are blessed of the Lord. (Isaiah 65:23)

CHILDREN

Because I keep Your statutes and commandments, Lord, it is well with me and my children. We prolong our days upon the earth. (Deuteronomy 4:40)

As for me and my house, we do serve the Lord. (Joshua 24:15)

God's tender mercies hover over my children. (Psalm 145:9)

I am a covenant partner with the Lord. His Spirit is in me. He has put His Words in my mouth. They do not depart from me, my seed, or future generations. (Isaiah 59:21)

The Lord has set before me life and death, blessing and cursing. I have chosen life that both I and my seed will live. (Deuteronomy 30:19)

Jesus was manifested to destroy all the works of the devil. Satan, <u>all</u> your works are destroyed in my children's lives. (I John 3:8)

No child in our family shall die and none of us shall die before our time. (Isaiah 65:20)

My children have no fellowship with darkness. They keep themselves from everything and everyone that appears to be evil. They hold fast to the good things of the Lord. (Ephesians 5:11; I Thessalonians 5:21,22)

I refrain my voice from weeping and my eyes from tears; God promises my work shall be rewarded and my children shall return from the hand of the enemy. (Jeremiah 31:16)

I am not ashamed nor disappointed, nor do I fear concerning any of my children or grandchildren. I see them sanctifying, fearing and praising God. The ones that err in spirit, come to understanding and the ones that rebel, learn the doctrine of God's Word. (Isaiah 29:22-24; Hebrews 6:1-2)

God's Words are in my heart and I teach them diligently to my children. Lord, Your Word is evident in my conversation, in the way I conduct myself and in the manner in which I handle all the affairs of my life. (Deuteronomy 6:6,7)

CHILDREN

My children are disciples taught of You, Lord; they are obedient to Your Word and great is their peace. I praise You, Lord, that Your angels have charge over them and keep them in all their ways. In their pathway is life, health, prosperity, abundance and safety and there is no death, sickness, poverty, lack or danger. I thank You, Lord, that because my children obey You, they are the head and not the tail, they are above only and not beneath. They are continual testimonies of Your greatness and mercy. (Isaiah 54:13; Psalm 91:11; Proverbs 12:28; Deuteronomy 28:13)

We are blessed of You, Lord. You increase us more and more. (Psalm 115:14,15)

I believe on the Lord, Jesus Christ; I am saved and so is my household. (Acts 16:31)

WORDS OF FAITH FOR CHILDREN

Children need to be trained to speak the Word. It is important that they know and understand what the Word says about their situations and circumstances. We suggest that you begin teaching your children one or two Scriptures every day, adding others gradually. Let your children learn by instruction, as well as example. Teach them to act on, or be doers of the Word.

By Jesus' stripes, I am healed. (Isaiah 53:5)

The Lord is my shepherd, I do not want. (Psalm 23:1)

No weapon formed against me prospers. (Isaiah 54:17)

I thank You, Lord, that You are instructing, teaching and guiding me by Your Holy Spirit in the way I should go. (Psalm 32:8)

I increase in wisdom, stature and favor with God and man, as Jesus did. (Luke 2:52)

Jesus is made unto me wisdom, I am smart in school. (I Corinthians 1:30)

I belong to Jesus and satan has no power over me. I am not overcome by evil, but I overcome evil with good. (Romans 12:21)

I am more than a conqueror in Jesus. (Romans 8:37)

I am of God. I am an overcomer because greater is He that is in me, than he that is in the world. (I John 4:4)

I obey my parents in all things, this pleases the Lord and I have long life. (Ephesians 6:1-3)

WORDS OF FAITH FOR CHILDREN

In my pathway is life and there is no death, destruction, poverty, lack, sickness or disease. Angels have charge over me to keep me in all my ways. (Psalm 16:11; 91:11)

I continue to increase in the knowledge of God. (Colossians 1:10,11)

The joy of the Lord is my strength. (Nehemiah 8:10)

I do what God's Word says and I am blessed in everything I do. (James 1:22,25)

I submit myself to God; I resist the devil and he flees from me. (James 4:7)

God has given me wisdom, knowledge and skill in learning. (Daniel 1:17)

I can do all things through Christ, because He gives me my strength. (Philippians 4:13)

Thank You Father, You forgive me for all the wrong things I do. You heal all sickness or disease that tries to come upon me. (Psalm 103:2,3)

I love Jesus and I do what His Word says. (John 14:15)

I walk in love as Christ did. (Ephesians 5:2)

God's Word says do not be afraid, so I do not fear. (John 14:27)

I forgive others because God's Word tells me to. I forgive them for the wrong things they do and say and God forgives me. (Mark 11:25)

God has not given me the spirit of fear. I have power, love and a sound mind. (II Timothy 1:7)

I have grace and favor with God, my principal, teachers, classmates, schoolmates, bus drivers, family and friends. (Luke 2:52)

Racism, prejudice, violence and discrimination are far from me in Jesus' name. (Job 22:28)

I trust God. I believe Him and I will not be ashamed. (Romans 10:11)

God is love. I know God and His love and I do not hate. (I John 4:8)

I show God's love through my words, my actions and my truthfulness. (I John 3:18)

WORDS OF FAITH FOR CHILDREN

My appetite, weight, height, health, and abilities are as God would have them to be. (Job 22:28)

I have the mind of Christ. (I Corinthians 2:16)

I am not afraid, for God is with me. I am not discouraged for He is my God; He gives me strength and helps me. (Isaiah 41:10)

I seek You, Lord and I understand all things. (Proverbs 28:5)

Thank you, Father, for giving me wisdom, knowledge and understanding of all subjects. (Daniel 1:4)

I refuse to take drugs, drink alcohol or smoke. My body is the temple of the Holy Spirit and dedicated to God. (I Corinthians 3:16)

Jesus is Lord over every test I take. I see and understand the questions and have supernatural recall of the correct answers to every question. (Job 22:28)

I am strong spiritually, alert mentally and grow up strong physically without any sickness or disease. (Job 22:25)

ABUNDANCE

I am transformed by the renewing of my mind. I demonstrate His good and perfect will. Therefore, I am prospering and in health even as my soul prospers. (Romans 12:2; III John :2)

My abundance is a supply for the needs of others. I sow bountifully, therefore I reap bountifully. (II Corinthians 8:14; 9:6)

God makes all grace abound toward me. I always have all sufficiency in all things. I tithe, give offerings, and give to the poor. My needs are met, my wants are supplied. I have enough left over to give into every other work as God directs. (II Corinthians 9:8)

I am a tither and God opens the windows of heaven and pours out blessings upon me. He rebukes the devourer for my sake. (Malachi 3:10,11)

I listen, see, speak and do what God's Word says. His blessings come upon me and overtake me. The Lord gives me an abundance in all things. He blesses the fruit of my body, my ground and everything I set my hand to. (Deuteronomy 28:1,2,4,8)

Jesus came to give us abundant life. We believe we have received it. (Mark 11:24; II Corinthians 4:13)

The Lord says I reap what I sow. I sow the Word and I refuse to receive anything contrary to It. (Galatians 6:7)

PROSPERITY

Most people think of prosperity as a financial condition. True prosperity is being successful and prospering in every area of life; spiritually, physically, mentally, materially, socially and financially. God prospers us so our abundance will fund the end time harvest, feed the poor and help those in need.

I am faithful over a little and God makes me ruler over much. (Matthew 25:21)

I do not trust in the uncertainty of money. I put my trust in God. He gives me all things to enjoy. (I Timothy 6:17)

The Lord, my God, teaches me to profit and leads me in the way I should go. (Isaiah 48:17)

I am blessed because I fear (reverence) the Lord, and delight greatly in His commandments. Wealth and riches are in my house, ministry and business, and my righteousness endures forever. (Psalm 112:1,3)

I keep the words of God's covenant and do them. I prosper in all that I do. (Deuteronomy 29:9)

I give to the poor and I do not lack. (Proverbs 28:27)

I seek first the kingdom of God and His righteousness, and all other things are added unto me. (Matthew 6:33)

I honor my Lord with all that I have and with the tithe of all my increase. I have more than enough and do not ever lack in any area. (Proverbs 3:9,10)

I am willing and obedient, therefore, I do eat the good of the land. (Isaiah 1:19)

I ALWAYS speak God's Word. I meditate in It day and night, seeing and doing what It says. I make my way prosperous and I have good success in everything I do. (Joshua 1:8)

I am blessed because I walk not in the counsel of the ungodly, nor stand in the way of sinners, nor sit in the seat of the scornful. I delight in God's law and meditate in It day and night. Everything I do prospers. (Psalm 1:1-3)

I obey and serve the Lord. My days are prosperous and my years are pleasant. (Job 36:11)

I give and it is given unto me. According to the measure I give, it is returned to me. I sow bountifully therefore, I reap bountifully. I give cheerfully and God makes all grace abound toward me that I have all sufficiency in all things. I have an abundance to give into every good work. (Luke 6:38; II Corinthians 9:6-8)

PROSPERITY

I do what the Lord my God says. I walk in His ways, keep His statutes and His testimonies. I prosper in whatever I do and wherever I go. (I Kings 2:3)

I abide in Jesus and His Word abides in me; I ask what I will according to His Word and it is done unto me. Our business, church and ministry prospers even as we do. (John 15:7)

I speak God's Word. It <u>NEVER</u> returns to Him void. It <u>ALWAYS</u> accomplishes what He pleases. He desires that I prosper and be in health even as my soul prospers. My soul is prospering, therefore, I am prospering and in good health. (Isaiah 55:11; III John :2)

I have no lack, for my God supplies all my needs according to His riches in glory by Christ Jesus. (Philippians 4:19)

Let the Lord be magnified. He has pleasure in the prosperity of His servant; Abraham's blessings are mine. (Psalm 35:27; Galatians 3:14)

The Lord is my shepherd, I do not want. (Psalm 23:1)

Jesus came that I would have life more abundantly and I do. (John 10:10)

I walk uprightly before the Lord and He withholds no good thing from me. I delight myself in my Lord and He gives me the desires of my heart. That desire is to be debt free that I might fund the end time harvest. (Psalm 37:4; Psalm 84:11)

Christ has redeemed me from the curse of the law; for sickness He has given me health, for poverty He has given me wealth, and for death He has given me eternal life. (Galatians 3:13; Deuteronomy 28: ; Galatians 4:5)

I hear, speak and do all that God tells me to, therefore, He opens unto me His good treasure. He blesses all the work of my hands, and I have an abundance to lend unto others. I do not have to borrow. I am the head and not the tail, above only and not beneath. (Deuteronomy 28:12,13)

Yours, Lord, is the greatness, the power, the glory, the victory and the majesty. All that is in heaven and earth is Yours. You are exalted as head above all. Riches and honor come of You. Power and might are in Your hand to make great and to give strength. I believe I receive according to Your Word. (I Chronicles 29:11,12)

PROSPERITY

I am an heir according to God's promise to Abraham and all his blessings are mine. They come upon me and overtake me, as I listen, observe and do what God says. Blessed is the fruit of my ground (house, business, ministry), my body (my children); everything I have is blessed. I am blessed in the city, the field, my daily provision, my future needs, when I come in and when I go out. God blesses everything I set my hand to. (Galatians 3:29; Deuteronomy 28:2-6)

EMPLOYMENT

Lord, I thank You that You hasten Your Word to perform It. You supply my every need, therefore, my need for the perfect job is met. (Jeremiah 1:12; Philippians 4:19)

The labor of my hands provides our food; we are happy and it is well with us. (Psalm 128:2)

The Word says increase comes by working. I am honest, I work and I increase financially. My work is a gift of God and I rejoice in it. (Ecclesiastes 5:19)

I delight myself in the Lord and He gives me the desires of my heart. The desire of my heart is for employment and I thank Him for providing the perfect job. I trust in the Lord and do good; I dwell in the land and I am fed. (Psalm 37:4,3)

The Lord is my sun and shield; He gives me grace and glory. He withholds no good thing from me because I walk uprightly. He provides the perfect job for me. (Psalm 84:11)

My God supplies my every need according to His riches in glory which are abundant and without end in Christ Jesus. I thank You, Father, I believe that I receive the perfect job with the right hours and the best salary, in Jesus' name. (Philippians 4:19; Mark 11:24)

Lord, Your Word says that where two or more on earth agree as touching anything they shall ask, it shall be done. Right now, we agree as touching a job; we believe we receive the perfect job with the best salary possible and we thank You for it in Jesus' name. (Matthew 18:19)

We thank You, Father, that no one in our family is now, nor ever shall be unemployed. Each has the perfect job in the right place, with the best salary, excellent working conditions and grace and favor with his employer. (Job 22:28)

EMPLOYMENT

Lord, I refuse to fear about finding a job. Through prayer, with thanksgiving, I tell You my requests concerning employment. Your peace, through Christ Jesus, keeps my heart and mind at rest as I wait on You for the manifestation of it. (Philippians 4:6,7)

I trust You, Lord with all my heart and lean not to my own understanding. In everything I do, I acknowledge You and You direct my paths to the best employment. (Proverbs 3:5,6)

God desires that I prosper and be in health even as my soul prospers. My soul is prospering, therefore, I am healthy and prospering with employment. (III John :2)

Father, Your Word says You know my works; You have set before me an open door that no man can close. I thank You for the open door of employment. (Revelation 3:8)

I do not fear, for You, Lord, are with me. I am not dismayed for You are my God. You strengthen me and help me to find the perfect job, with the best salary, hours and working conditions. (Isaiah 41:10)

Jesus increased in wisdom and stature and in favor with God and man and so do I. I claim favor as I seek employment. (Luke 2:52)

Rain and snow come down from heaven and water the earth causing it to give seed to the sower and bread to the eater. Lord, through this job, You provide me with seed to sow and bread to eat. I thank You for it in Jesus' name. (Isaiah 55:10,11)

BUSINESS, ETC.

(These scriptures may be spoken for individuals, families, ministries, and churches, as well as businesses.)

We speak God's Word. We meditate and consider It day and night; because we do all that is written therein, we make our way prosperous and have good success in our company. (Joshua 1:8)

We trust in the Lord with all our hearts and lean not to our own understanding. We acknowledge Him in all our ways and He directs us in every area of this company. (Proverbs 3:5,6)

We obey and serve God, therefore, our businesses have prosperous days and years of pleasures. (Job 36:11)

You are the Lord our God who teaches us to profit and leads our company in the way it should go. (Isaiah 48:17)

We operate in mercy and truth. We have grace and favor with God and everyone we meet, including our customers, other companies we deal with and our creditors. (Proverbs 3:3,4)

We have willing and skillful Christian workers for every manner of service and all manner of workmanship in this company. (I Chronicles 28:21)

God maintains our right and our cause of this business at all times and in every matter, so the world may know He is God and there is no other. (I Kings 8:59,60)

It is not by might, nor by power that this corporation prospers, but by Your Spirit. We fear the Lord and delight in His commandments. We are blessed. Wealth and riches are in our houses and businesses. (Psalm 112:1-3)

We, in this company, are good people. We show favor and lend. We guide our affairs with discretion. (Psalm 112:5)

God promises He will supply our company's every need according to His riches in glory by Christ Jesus. Lord, since Your riches are without end, our every need is met. (Philippians 4:19)

We wait on You, Lord and we are never ashamed. This company prospers and is a glory unto You! (Isaiah 49:23; Job 22:28)

Lord, I believe Your Word which says, he that has pity on the poor lends unto You and You will repay him again. We have pitied the poor and we thank You that You repay that which we have given. (Proverbs 19:17)

BUSINESS, ETC.

Lord, Your Word says, he that gives to the poor shall not lack. We have given to the poor individually as well as corporately. We thank You that according to Your Word, neither we, nor our company, ever lack in any area. (Proverbs 28:27; Luke 1:38)

We are blessed because we always consider the poor. The Lord continually delivers our company from all trouble. He preserves our company and keeps it alive. We are blessed and He does not deliver us into the will of those who want to see us fail. (Psalm 41:1-2)

Riches and honor come of You, Lord. You reign over all. Power and might are in Your hand to make great and to give strength. We thank You and praise Your glorious name that the future of this company is in Your hand. (I Chronicles 29:12,13)

We have knowledge, skill and wisdom in business and are led by the Holy Spirit. We are good stewards of the money God provides for our company and we use wisdom in spending. (Daniel 1:17; James 3:13; Luke 12:42,43)

Lord, You make us glad through Your work; our company triumphs in the works of Your hands. (Psalm 92:4)

We remain fixed, trusting in the Lord. We are not afraid of bad news. We overcome every situation with the blood of Jesus and the Word of God spoken out of our mouths as a testimony. (Psalm 112:7; Revelation 12:11)

We thank You, Lord. You always cause this company to triumph in Christ Jesus. (II Corinthians 2:14)

God instructs us and shows us the way we should go. He guides us in all our business affairs. (Psalm 32:8)

We fear (reverence) the Lord and delight in His commandments. We are blessed. Wealth and riches are in our houses and businesses. (Psalm 112:1-3)

FOR PASTORS

Our pastor is a servant of the Lord who does not strive. He is gentle and patiently teaches all. (II Timothy 2:24-26)

Our pastor is a vessel of honor, sanctified, prepared, and available to be used for every good work of the Lord. (II Timothy 2:21)

Our pastor is strong in the grace of the Anointed Jesus. He teaches the things of God. He is a teacher of teachers. (II Timothy 2:1-2)

Our pastor works among us, is over us in the Lord and is highly esteemed in love. (I Thessalonians 5:12,13)

Our pastor gives himself continually to prayer and to the ministry of the Word. (Acts 6:4)

The Lord gives our pastor boldness to speak His Word; healings and signs and wonders follow as the Holy Spirit wills. (Acts 4:29-30)

Our pastor believes God and is careful to maintain good works. He has the gifts of the Holy Spirit, operating in his life to profit everyone. (Titus 3:8; I Corinthians 12:7)

Our pastor doesn't walk in the counsel of the ungodly, doesn't stand in the way of sinners and doesn't sit in the seat of the scornful. He delights himself in the Word and meditates in It day and night. Everything he does, prospers. (Psalm 1:1-3)

The Spirit of the Lord is in our Pastor. The Lord has anointed him to preach the Good News. Signs and wonders follow his teaching of the Word. He lays hands on the sick and they recover, he casts out demons and is used in the gifts of the Holy Ghost. (Isaiah 61:1; Mark 16:15-18; I Corinthians 12:7-11)

PRAISE

In You, Lord God, do I praise Your Word. (Psalm 56:10)

My lips continually praise You because Your loving kindness is better than life. I bless You while I live, I lift up my hands in Your name. (Psalm 63:3,4)

You are blessed Lord; You are the God of Your people. You only do wondrous things; blessed is Your glorious name forever. Let the whole earth be filled with Your glory; Amen and Amen. (Psalm 72:18,19)

PRAISE

Lord, I will sing of Your mercies forever; I speak continually of Your faithfulness to all generations. (Psalm 89:1)

Blessed is the Lord, Who lives! You are my Rock. I exalt You, God of my salvation. (Psalm 18:46)

Lord, I praise You with my whole heart; I tell of Your marvelous works. I am glad and rejoice in You. I sing praises to Your name, Oh Most High. My enemies are turned back and perish at Your presence. (Psalm 9:1-3)

I call on You Lord; You save me from my enemies. You are worthy to be praised. (II Samuel 22;4)

I praise Your name Lord, for Your name alone is excellent. Your glory is above heaven and earth. (Psalm 148:13)

Oh Lord, Yours is the greatness and the power, the glory, the victory and the majesty. All that is in the heaven and earth is Yours. Yours is the kingdom and You are exalted above all. Both riches and honor come from You; You reign over all, and in Your hand is the power to make great and give strength to all. We thank You and praise Your glorious name. (I Chronicles 29:11-13)

VICTORY

I set my will that my mouth does not speak wrongly; I say only what the Word says, and that keeps me from the paths of the destroyer. (Psalm 17:3,4)

Because I am a tither, the Lord rebukes the devourer for my sake. He contends with those who contend with me. (Malachi 3:11; Isaiah 49:25)

My righteousness is of You, Lord and this is my heritage that no weapon formed against me shall prosper and every tongue that rises against me is condemned. (Isaiah 54:17)

I am not afraid nor dismayed at the multitude against me, for the battle is not mine, but the Lord's. (II Chronicles 20:15)

The Lord has delivered me out of the hand of the mighty, out of the hand of the strong and He continues to deliver me out of your hand, satan. (I Samuel 17:37)

I am born of God and overcome the world. My faith is the victory that overcomes the world. (I John 5:4)

VICTORY

Lord, You have redeemed me and call me by my name. I am Yours. When I go through waters (trouble) and through rivers (difficulties) they do not overflow me for You are with me. When I walk through fire (oppression) I am not burned, because You are always with me. (Isaiah 43:1,2)

Thank You Lord, You always cause me to triumph in Christ Jesus. (II Corinthians 2:14)

Lord, You rebuke the ungodly and destroy the wicked. You always maintain my right and my cause. (Psalm 9:5,4)

I am persuaded that neither death nor life, nor angels, nor principalities, nor powers nor things present nor things to come, nor height, nor depth, nor any person or thing is able to separate me from God's love which is in Christ Jesus. (Romans 8:38,39)

All things are mine; things of men, things of the world, things of life and death, things present and things to come. All are mine because I am Christ's and He is God's. (I Corinthians 3:21-23)

No good thing which the Lord has spoken fails; all come to pass. (Joshua 21:45)

There is none like You, Lord. You are glorious in holiness, fearful in praises and doing wonders. (Exodus 15:11)

Jesus came to earth as a human and became sin for me. He took my place on the cross. Through His death, He destroyed the devil who had the power of death. (Hebrews 2:14)

I do not war with people; the weapons of my warfare are not carnal, but mighty through God to pull down every stronghold. I cast down imaginations, and every thought that attempts to take the place of my knowledge of God and His Word. I take every thought which is contrary to the Word and bring it back into obedience to Christ and His Word. I make the Word final authority in my life. (II Corinthians 10:3-5)

God promises that I have life in Christ Jesus; whatever I go through I am not ashamed, because I believe in Him, and I know He is able to keep everything I give to Him. (II Timothy 1:1,12)

No weapon formed against me prospers; and every tongue that rises in judgment against me, is condemned. (Isaiah 54:17)

The peace of God keeps my heart and mind through Jesus. (Philippians 4:17)

The angel of the Lord is with me and delivers me. (Psalm 34:7)

PROTECTION
When I pass through waters of trouble, You are with me. When I walk through rivers, they do not cover me. When I walk through fire, I shall not be burned. (Isaiah 43:1,2)

USING THE BLOOD OF JESUS
I cover myself and all my family, my home, my vehicles, business, company, church, our finances, health, marriage, successes, victories, all of my possessions, everything and everyone that concerns us with the blood of Jesus. I claim the Father's divine protection upon us from every attack of all spirits of darkness and satan, himself. I bring the power of the blood of Jesus and His mighty name against you, satan to bind you away from everything that concerns us. I loose the power of the blood and His name to fulfill all that the Word promises in our lives, now!

I recognize this to be an attack from you, satan and I refuse it with the blood of Jesus. I declare the blood of Jesus overcomes you satan, and I apply it right now to this situation. You are defeated.

I apply the blood of Jesus to _____. This is a part of the curse of the law and we have been redeemed from that curse by the shed blood of Jesus.

I place the blood of Jesus as a witness over my home, business, ministry, church, etc. I believe in my heart and say with my mouth that I trust totally in my Father, His Word, the name of Jesus and His blood. I do not fear. I am not moved. I have victory in every situation and the blood of Jesus is my guarantee.

In the name of Jesus and His blood we will not be victims of, part of, witnesses to any crimes, violence, racist or terrorist attacks, acts of violence, racism, prejudice, discrimination, or hate crimes. No weapon formed against us prospers. No harm comes near us and no evil befalls us.

In the name of Jesus and His shed blood there will be no transfer of evil spirits to anyone of us from any source whatsoever. I have a covenant with my Father, through the blood of Jesus, which can not be broken and never ends.

I apply the blood of Jesus to all vehicles we or our loved ones ride in, from front to back, side to side, inside and outside, top to bottom, and every working part. We will not be witness to or any part of any accident or injury, minor, major, or fatal, no flat tires, breakdowns, car jacking. We leave and return safely with no problems whatsoever.

I hold the blood of Jesus over myself, my family, those I pray for, the church, my ministry, etc. for protection against every evil person, every evil spirit, every evil thing, and every evil plan of satan.

I cover myself, my family, and everything that concerns us with the blood of Jesus and claim the Father's divine protection upon us. We overcome by the blood of the Lamb and the Word of our testimony.

Sickness, disease, poverty, lack, death, failure, destruction are all part of the curse of the law. We have been redeemed by the blood of Jesus. I say it, stand on it, and I overcome you satan in every one of these areas by the blood of Jesus. The Word is my witness, all of Heaven is my witness, and the blood is my witness that you have no right to attack me or my seed. The blood of Jesus has defeated you.

PSALM 91

God's Word must become such a part of us, that we respond to each situation and circumstance with what the Word says. Psalm 91 is God's promise of divine protection. When we meet His conditions (living in His Word and staying so close to Him we are in His shadow), we are eligible for His divine protection.

I dwell (live, abide) in the secret place of the Most High God. I abide (live, dwell) in the shadow of the Almighty. (verse 1)

Lord, You are my fortress, my God, my refuge, my hiding place, my escape from danger. In You, and You alone, do I trust. I do not trust in anyone or anything else. (verse 2)

Absolutely, You Lord deliver me from the hidden traps, temptations and seductions of satan. You save me from sickness and disease that neither drugs nor doctors can cure (noisome pestilence). (verse 3)

PSALM 91

You protect and keep me as a mother hen keeps her chicks under her wings. The truth of Your Word is my protection and armor. (verse 4)

I am not afraid of the terrors of darkness (abductions, rapes, robberies, evils that happen at night). I am not afraid of arrows that fly by day (riots, attacks, wars, etc.) (verse 5)

I am not afraid of the pestilence (plagues, infections, deadly diseases) from satan's realm of darkness nor of the destructions that come during the day (recession, fire, floods, earthquakes, etc.) (verse 6)

A thousand may fall beside me and ten thousand around me may be destroyed by sickness, disease, wars, storms, violence, fire, hurricanes, etc., but destruction will not come near me because my total trust is in You, Lord. You keep and sustain me! (verse 7)

I see the reward of the wicked (total defeat), and my victory through Jesus. (verse 8)

Because I have made You my refuge, Lord and You, Most High, my dwelling place, no harm comes near me, no evil befalls me, no plague or calamity comes near my home, family, business or ministry, etc. (verses 9, 10)

You command Your angels to keep me in all my ways. They keep, protect and surround me at all times, everywhere I go. (verse 11)

Those angels lift me up in their hands even for the slightest touch of my foot hitting a stone. (verse 12)

I tread upon the lion (the powerful), and the adder (the deadly). The young lion (the strong) and the dragon (satan himself), I trample under my feet. (verse 13)

I have set my love upon You and You, Lord deliver me. You set me on high because I have known Your name. (verse 14)

I call upon You and You answer me. You are with me in trouble; You deliver me and honor me. (verse 15)

You satisfy me with long life and show me Your salvation (victory, deliverance, healing, prosperity, etc.). (verse 16)